Let's Be Revolting

A Study of the Magnificat

Compiled by Ann Bird and Stuart Burgess

Let's Be Revolting

©1999 Trustees for Methodist Church Purposes

Published by Methodist Publishing House

ISBN 1 85852 107 6

Contents

The Magnificat

My soul glorifies the Lord,
My spirit rejoices in God my Saviour!

For he has blessed me lavishly
And makes me ready to respond.

He shatters my little world
And lets me be poor before him.

He takes from me all my plans
And gives me more than I can hope for or ask.

He gives me opportunities and the ability
to become free and to burst through my boundaries.

He gives me the strength to be daring,
To build on him alone, for he shows himself
as the ever greater One in my life.

He has made known to me this:
It is in my being servant
That it becomes possible
For God's kingdom to break through
Here and now.

(Translation by Sr Olga Wanke IBVM from German)

Preface

We have chosen this version of Mary's Magnificat in the hope that its language will shed fresh light on the challenge that is implied in its words. For although the Magnificat is a song of joy and thankfulness it is also a recognition of the cost of accepting God's blessing and call.

Like Mary, we who rejoice in God's love and who recognise him as our Saviour, cannot simply rest in that personal assurance, crucial though it is. We are called, as Mary was, to be among those who help to change the world, to prepare the way for God to bring in the kingdom. We are, indeed, called 'to be revolting' in God's Name on behalf of all those who feel themselves to be beyond God's love or who are disadvantaged in any way.

The Magnificat can be read on many levels. We invite you to share it with us from this particular perspective and hope that it will not only bring fresh insights but will evoke a response which helps you, too, to 'become free' and to have 'the strength to be daring' in his Name. Mary was prepared to put herself on the line for God. Are you?

Ann Bird

1 *My soul glorifies the Lord,*
My spirit rejoices in God my Saviour!
For he has blessed me lavishly
And makes me ready to respond.

The Magnificat is a song of Messianic joy which speaks of the greatness, the majesty and the might of God, and of the ways in which his kindness and justice are given to the people of Israel, and in particular to Mary through the birth of Jesus.

The Magnificat, Benedictus and Nunc Dimittis derive their names from the fourth century Latin Vulgate Version of the Bible. All three songs are based on biblical texts, and the Magnificat echoes the song of Hannah in 1 Samuel 2:1-10:

Hannah prayed and said,

My heart exults in the Lord; my strength is exalted in my God.
My mouth derides my enemies, because I rejoice in my victory.

There is no Holy One like the Lord, no one besides you;
there is no Rock like our God.

Talk no more so very proudly,
let not arrogance come from your mouth;
for the Lord is a God of knowledge, and by him actions are weighed.

The bows of the mighty are broken, but the feeble gird on strength.

Those who were full have hired themselves out for bread,
but those who were hungry are fat with spoil.
The barren has borne seven, but she who has many children is forlorn.

The Lord kills and brings to life; he brings down to Sheol and raises up.

The Lord makes poor and makes rich; he brings low, he also exalts.

He raises up the poor from the dust; and he lifts the needy
from the ash heap,
to make them sit with princes and inherit a seat of honour.
For the pillars of the earth are the Lord's, and on them he has
set the world.

He will guard the feet of his faithful ones, but the wicked shall
be cut off in darkness;
for not by might does one prevail.

The Lord! His adversaries shall be shattered; the Most High
will thunder in heaven.
The Lord will judge the ends of the earth; he will give
strength to his king,
and exalt the power of his anointed.

The Song of Hannah provides Mary with the starting point for her own Magnificat. In it she praises God for the miraculous way in which he has touched her own life, at the same time acknowledging his faithfulness to the generations of the people of Israel from Abraham onwards, who have seen his continuing justice and mercy.

The past tense is used — not to describe God's past care for the downtrodden — but because God has already taken decisive action in the promised sending of his Son. In Mary the past and the present come together, forming a bridge between the old and new order. Mary is the vehicle of the love of God. In the Service of Holy Communion there is a similar bringing together of the past and present. In the Great Prayer of Thanksgiving we remember what God has done for us in the past and we experience it in the present.

When a General Election is held in Britain each major political party publishes its manifesto. It sets out (clearly or otherwise) its objectives and the way ahead for the next few years. The Magnificat reads almost as a manifesto; it incorporates a new way of life in which the values of the world are turned upside down. Jesus develops this theme when he visits the synagogue in Nazareth, described in Luke 4:16:

When he came to Nazareth, where he had been brought up,
he went to the synagogue on the sabbath day, as was his
custom. He stood up to read, and the scroll of the prophet
Isaiah was given to him. He unrolled the scroll and found
the place where it was written:

'The Spirit of the Lord is upon me, because he has anointed me to bring good news to the poor.

He has sent me to proclaim release to the captives and recovery of sight to the blind, to let the oppressed go free, to proclaim the year of the Lord's favour.'

In some ways the Lukan narrative of Jesus' visit to the synagogue is an extension of the Magnificat. For centuries the Jews had lived under foreign occupation and tyranny – which allowed no one to grow rich and powerful except the collaborators. 'The poor' had become almost a technical term for the faithful adherents of the Law who trusted in God alone for their ultimate deliverance. There is also a close association with the Beatitudes in Matthew 5 in which Jesus declares the poor to be blessed. Luke, in his Gospel, takes up this revolutionary theme and emphasises Jesus' ministry to the poor and the sick.

The Magnificat is timeless in its meaning and application.

It speaks to us:
1. of humility
2. of justice
3. of revolution
4. of engagement.

1. Mary's life is one of humility and she is the vehicle of the love of God. St Teresa of Avila speaks to us of the gift of humility and says, 'By humility God allows himself to be conquered.' Humility is needed as we enter the 21st century for it is important to realise that, however technologically advanced we are, we do not possess all the answers to the world's problems.

2. Justice speaks to us of Christ's concern for the poor, the outcast and women in society. T. S. Eliot writes about the 'freedom to dare' and the need to challenge the values of society, especially in terms of power and status. We should show concern, as Jesus did, for the broken and vulnerable.

3. The Magnificat speaks to us of revolution. It challenges us to make connections between our personal faith and the faith we proclaim to an ever-changing world. We live in a complex and evolving society but the Incarnation proclaims that God has come in Christ to our confused and hurting world. The Gospel must

continue to challenge people and confront them with issues such as social justice, poverty and wealth creation.

4. The Magnificat challenges us to be included and known in the over-arching purposes of God. In the same way as a picture can be made up of thousands of dots, each differing in colour, density and application, so we, the people of God are all part of God's overall 'picture' to which we contribute in unique, individual ways.

The Magnificat is a promise that, in the love of God, we are affirmed, held and united. But it also challenges us, as individuals, as the community of the Church, and as members of the society in which we live.

Discussion Starters

1. How would you define 'glory'?

2. Following on from the Magnificat what are the priorities for the Church in the 21st century?

3. How can we make connection between the Gospel and society?

Stuart Burgess

Full of grace . . .
I wonder what that felt like.
Was your acceptance swift
And total, meek as your
Stained glass image?
Or was it wrung from you
In sweat and agony of mind?
The God I know does not get
Submissions very easily,
But then I'm not a Saint.
Perhaps you weren't either,
Just an ordinary person,
Struggling to understand.
Has the adulation over the years
Been a bit of an embarrassment,
Imprisoning you in dogma,
Preventing us from seeing you
As you are?

The family, were they convinced?
And the neighbours? I've often
Wondered about that visit to
Elisabeth — was that to get you
Away from all the gossip, until
The wedding could be arranged
Discreetly? And what about Joseph?
He must have thought it
A fine kind of angel who'd visited you.

We'll never know — but whatever
Happened, I'm pretty sure
The sword that pierced your soul
Didn't wait for the crucifixion.
And I've got a feeling that
You watch with some sympathy
As we struggle with our
Mysteries and pain.

Ann Lewin

Christ, through whom all things were made,
sustain all creation.

Christ, exalted in the lowest and the least,
give us humility.

Christ, present in the poor and the oppressed,
fill us with compassion.

Christ, forsaken in the hungry and the homeless,
minister to them through our hands.

Christ, present where two or three are gathered,
be known among us.

Christ, present in word, sacrament and sign,
grant us your peace.

The Methodist Worship Book

Vulnerable God,
you challenge the powers that rule this world
through the needy, the compassionate,
and those who are filled with longing.
Make us hunger and thirst to see right prevail,
and single-minded in seeking peace;
that we may see your face
and be satisfied in you,
through Jesus Christ. Amen.

Janet Morley

2 He shatters my little world
And lets me be poor before him.
He takes from me all my plans
And gives more than I can hope for or ask.

In his poem 'To a Mouse', Robert Burns paints a picture of life which many of us experience at one time or another:

> The best-laid schemes o' mice an' men
> Gang aft agley.

We are vulnerable to shattering experiences.

There are occasions when, however carefully we make arrangements for a particular event, the unexpected can happen. In the paraphrase of the Magnificat, it is God who enters our 'little world' and overturns all our plans. The question then arises, do all changes come from God or are there human elements within them? In life we continually interact with other people. Some of these interactions will result in changes in our lives, and we can and do get upset when plans go wrong or are changed.

Most of us have lived through 'shattering' experiences. There are some people, however, whose experiences can only be described as devastating. One couple, having lived through the disappointment of two miscarriages, were eagerly awaiting the birth of their third child. The mother's labour was long and difficult and soon after the birth the parents were told that their little girl was severely handicapped. They were angry with God. Why had he allowed this to happen? Where was his love for them? There were times when they wondered if more could have been done to protect their child, and the mother, especially, felt a sense of failure. However, as time went by she discovered she was free to listen and support other mothers in similar circumstances. Her vulnerability in a time of weakness made her a resource for others.

God can and does speak to us through our thoughts and feelings and at times he may also use a person to make his will known to us. Mary heard him speak to her through his messenger. She could hardly have expected all her plans to be turned upside down so quickly. We do not know what her immediate reaction might have been on hearing that she was to become the mother of a special person, the One who would bring in the kingdom. She must have wondered how Joseph would respond to the news of her pregnancy. She was taking a risk of possible rejection when she replied to God's messenger:

> Here am I, the servant of the Lord; let it be with me according to your word.

Mary knew that life was going to be different. Any plans she had made, or any hopes she cherished in her heart, were changed. She accepted the opportunity to respond to a unique decision made for her, but as a wife and mother, living according to the customs of her time. Most of us are not expected to face such dramatic changes in our lives, but we do know what it means to have our carefully made plans disrupted. We don't like to lose control over our lives and when this happens we may feel frustrated or even insecure. The paraphrase of the Magnificat points out that God does not leave us with lives that are 'shattered'. His grace freely gives us the ability to 'be poor before him', and offers us 'more than we can hope for or ask'.

To be shattered can be a prelude to the possibility of being remade. The idea of being 'poor before God' is not, at first sight, something we easily accept. The Jews believed that the 'plenty' they enjoyed was a sign of God's favour. The writer of Deuteronomy describes how God will provide for them:

> Blessed shall you be in the city, and
> blessed shall you be in the field.
> Blessed shall be the fruit of your womb,
> the fruit of your ground, and the fruit
> of your livestock, both the increase of
> your cattle and the issue of your flock.
>
> Deuteronomy 28:3-4

The same God allows us 'to be poor before him.' Poor, in this context, does not refer to those who are economically disadvantaged, it describes those who recognise their total dependence upon God. Jesus reminds us that such 'poor' are blessed (Matthew 5:3). 'Blessed', from the Greek word 'makarios', is a difficult word to translate into English. Its meaning incorporates ideas of wholeness, of joy, of well-being, and of peace.

I have among my treasures a booklet commemorating the centenary of a small Methodist chapel, now no longer in existence. Some years ago the members joined in a covenant with their Anglican friends and the chapel was sold. There was joy in coming together but also pain at the loss of their place of worship and the personal memories associated with it. The organ had been donated by a relative of one of the members and the pulpit made by the great-grandfather of another. In giving up their little chapel the members were also giving up some of their past and were asked to go forward trusting in God. The faith of that small society and that shown by Mary is the kind of trust that God wants us to have in our lives. Mary, for example, was given no guarantees of her safety. She was not provided with an ideal place to give birth to her first child, nor was she given any assurance that caring for Jesus would be easy.

To trust God like that is an act of faith. Mary did not find this easy. Although she must have been a person of particular grace and openness to be chosen by God to bear his Son, in another sense we do her a disservice if we think of her as anything other than an ordinary Jewish woman, chosen and called to an extraordinary task. Some thirty years after that unforgettable experience of coming face to face with God's messenger, Mary is portrayed in the Gospels as still behaving like a normal mother. Concerned about Jesus' sanity and his safety, she came with some of her family to where Jesus was teaching and waited outside, hoping to speak with him. Jesus did not leave the crowd and come out to his family but asked the question 'Who is my mother, and who are my brothers?' (Matthew 12:48). He was making the point that we are all valued and included in his family if we do God's will.

We can only guess how Mary felt at that moment. Probably what disturbed her most was that her son appeared to be antagonistic towards the religious authorities of the time, people she held in high esteem. It was natural for a mother, anxious about her son's welfare, to want to protect him and take him home. We cannot criticise Mary because she did not fully understand. But when, like Mary, we too go through periods when we do not understand, when we become disillusioned or when we doubt, simple trust does not come easily. Yet such is the generosity of God that whatever life holds for us, he promises to give us 'more than (we) can hope for or ask'.

There must have been times in Mary's life when she felt hurt and misunderstood, yet she gave Jesus the stability and care that enabled him to love more widely. When she watched and waited at the cross while her son died, she would have remembered the words of Simeon:

'And a sword will pierce your own soul too' (Luke 2:35). However, she was counted among the believers and recorded as such in Acts 1:14. To be able, like Mary, to experience God's manifold blessing amid the twists and turns of life is a mystery for us as Christians to explore. Often we are so involved with what is happening to us we fail to recognise God working in our lives and showering us with his gifts. It is among the ordinary experiences of life, both good and bad, that God's blessings can be discovered.

Discussion Starters

1. When does God 'shatter' our 'little world' to help us turn and grow?

2. How much choice did women have in the time of Jesus?
    How much choice do women have in today's society?

3. Are we so concerned with the everyday events of our lives that we fail to notice God's gifts to us?

Margaret Hale

Dear God

We thank you
    that you whisper today
to everything in us that is tender and receptive,
everything that is deep and still –
finding the female
    in both man and women
    – asking to be conceived in us.

We thank you
    that you challenge today
everything in us that is pretentious and pompous,
everything that is high and mighty –
choosing the humble heart
    of both pauper and prince
    – asking to be carried by us.

We thank you
    that you reassure today
everything in us that doubts and questions,
everything that is troubled and anxious –
seeing through to the hunger
    in both fearful and faithful
    – asking to be nourished by us.

We thank you
    that you honour today
everything in us that labours and gives,
everything that suffers and strives –
dignifying the obedience
    of both weak and strong
    – asking to be born in us.

Kate Compston

Come humbly, Holy Child,
stir in the womb
of our complacency;
shepherd our vision
of the little we need
for abundant living.

Come humbly, Holy Spirit,
to whisper through the leaves
in the garden of our ignorance,
exposing our blindness
to children dying,
hungry and in pain.

Come humbly, Holy Light,
pierce our lack of generosity and love,
scattering our dark fear
of living freely in your way,
poured out in wanton service.

Come humbly, Holy Wisdom,
cry through the empty streets
of our pretence to care,
that the face of the poor
will be lifted up,
for holy is your name.

Come humbly, Holy God,
be born into our rejoicing,
Come quickly, humble God,
and reign.

From a Mothers' Union day on 'Magnificat', Durham 1989

3. *He gives me opportunities and the ability to become free and to burst through my boundaries.*

The time, Thursday, 4th December 1997; the place, King's College Chapel, London; the occasion, the Advent Carol Service. I sat listening to the carols and antiphons for Advent, many of which my husband and I had sung many years ago as members of the King's Chapel choir and the music evoked memories of people, of events, of the time that had passed since then. Yet in the midst of all the recollection I was conscious of how all the seemingly disconnected events were inextricably woven together. Past choices, past friendships, past opportunities – they were all part of who I was at that present moment and there was thankfulness, there was regret and there was a sense of incredulity that life had followed the pattern it had. It was all very nostalgic!

Then suddenly the mood changed. The choir burst into music I had never heard before. I was listening to Giles Swayne's 'Magnificat'. Gone were the soothing melodies, the 'religious' cadences. All of a sudden I was in a world of African rhythms, a kaleidoscope of sound and an overwhelming sense of vitality and expectancy. It was spellbinding, one of those indescribable experiences when you feel that all your perceptions have been heightened.

Now, in retrospect, I can fit those moments into the rest of that Carol Service and can see the whole as a parable of what God has made possible for me during the past 40 years from the time when I used to sing the Magnificat in that Chapel during Evensong every week. At that time the opportunities and choices ahead of me seemed boundless. Life was there for the taking and I expected to have a large measure of control over it. But the number of big opportunities for change or new beginnings have not been noticeably frequent! Those that have come my way have so often had to be seen in the light of other people's needs, other people's choices. Consequently opportunities have of necessity been more limited than I might have expected. In any case to respond to one opportunity inevitably means closing the door on others. To marry or to remain single, to have children, to work, to worship in a particular church – all are decisions which open up some opportunities and close down others. Life is not normally the sudden and unexpected outpouring of a Swayne 'Magnificat', rather it is the measured beat of the antiphon or the traditional melody.

It is in that 'ordinariness', the accustomed, that the greatest opportunities present themselves. As I look back, it is not the lack of opportunities that I regret. It is my timid attitude to many of them. The dictionary defines 'opportunity' as 'favourable juncture, good chance, opening' with the suggestion that opportunities have about them something beneficial to the person concerned, and it is easy to see how a new job, the making of a new friendship, the chance to travel, can be seen as an opportunity to be grasped and enjoyed. But even the most exciting opportunities carry with them the element of risk, and it is all too easy to choose one's cherished security in preference to anything that might interrupt or threaten the status quo. I have had to fight all my life against my perceived need for security and I am certain that at times life has been the poorer for it.

Mary was so different. She accepted the opportunity God had offered to her, though she must have been aware that her choice laid her wide open to the likelihood of pain and hurt as well as to blessing and fulfilment. And so it did. At the end of her life would she still have been able to say, 'He gives me the ability to become free and to burst through my boundaries'? By risking everything for God she had also risked humiliation as an unmarried mother, she had seen her son take a direction in life which at times made her feel rejected, she had been constrained to watch his agonising death at an early age. Was that the 'ability to become free', 'to burst through boundaries'? We do not know what Mary actually thought, but everything within our own experience would lead us to believe that the paradox for her would be the same as it is for us and that, for all the pain it involved, she would still have given thanks for the opportunity God had opened up for her. Clearly, too, she remained faithful, in spite of all the apparent evidence to the contrary, to the belief that God was working his purpose out in and through the life and death of Jesus. We know this because she is recorded as 'numbered among the believers' after Jesus' resurrection.

For most of us, most of the time, the greatest opportunities occur in the apparently little things of life, especially in the way in which we respond to what happens to us or to other people. Each day, in fact, is crammed with opportunities to become less selfish, to become more understanding, to become involved with those who need our support, to be gentle, to discover more of God in creation, to re-organise our priorities to see God's hand in our lives. Each day brings with it the possibility of discovering some new potential within ourselves, some new way of responding to circumstances, some gift we have not previously recognised. And every time we grasp such a moment positively we are in fact becoming freer. We are pushing out what we thought of as our limits and 'bursting our boundaries'. Moreover, our natural response becomes one of thankfulness and rejoicing because whatever else life may hold, in at least one respect life is good.

This is not to belittle or judge those who seem unable to 'break free'. God is as present for them as he is for those who find the strength to overcome their restrictions or hurts, their agonies of mind or body. In fact we believe in a Gospel which underlines God's preference for the vulnerable and the weak and those who have neither the strength nor motivation to struggle against the odds any longer.

Yet it is amazing that the people who seem to be hedged around by the most daunting boundaries so often seem to be most able to transcend those boundaries and show the way forward for the rest of us. I couldn't listen to Swayne's 'Magnificat' without relating the African rhythm to the courage and fortitude of the thousands of black people like Nelson Mandela who would not rest until freedom was a reality. I cannot speak with many of those who live with severe disability without being humbled by their indomitable spirit and their will to surmount all possible obstacles. Many in this world who appear to be most bound are in the most profound sense the most free.

The Bidding Prayer at the Advent Carol Service as quoted in the next paragraph did not specifically mention 'opportunities'. It spoke instead of 'waiting upon God' as Mary did, reminding us that only if we 'wait on him' can we hope to make the most of the opportunities that come to us. If we are open to God in this way, when opportunities do present themselves we shall be ready for them and respond appropriately. We shall also be able to look back with gratitude and look forward with expectancy as we acknowledge the presence of God in all our opportunities.

> We ask God to renew in us his gifts of hope and endurance.
> We wait with Mary in simplicity and readiness to obey the
> will of God. As we listen to the Gospel of the Annunciation
> may we too rejoice in the gift that comes by faith, Christ in
> us, the hope of glory. We wait in faith with the whole

Church of God in eager expectation for the completion of God's purposes, asking God to nourish us on our way to him by word and sacrament.

Discussion Starters:

1. What could 'becoming free' mean for you?

2. Mary risked everything for God. In what ways does our cautious (or in some cases overconfident!) attitude to life prevent us from responding to the opportunities that are there for us – in our worship, in our relationships, in our work situations?

3. Does our belief in Jesus' resurrection fill us with the enthusiasm to 'be revolting', to turn the world upside down in his name?

Ann Bird

O God, whose word is fruitless
when the mighty are not put down,
      the humble remain humiliated,
      the hungry are not filled,
      and the rich are:
make good your word,
and begin with us.
Open our hearts and unblock our ears
to hear the voices of the poor
and share their struggle;
and send us away empty with longing
for your promises to come true
in Jesus Christ. Amen.

Janet Morley

I believe in God
Who didn't create the world as something finished
as a thing which has to remain the same forever
who doesn't rule by eternal laws
which are irrevocable
nor by natural order of poor and rich
experts and uninformed
rulers and helpless.

I believe in God
who wants the conflict among the living
and the transformation of the existing
by our work
by our politics.

I believe in Jesus Christ
who was right when he
'an individual who cannot do anything'
like ourselves
worked on the transformation of all things in existence
and perished doing it.

Looking at him I realise
how our intelligence is crippled
our fantasy suffocated
our efforts wasted
because we don't live the way he lived.
Every day I fear
that he died in vain
because he is buried in our churches
because we have betrayed his revolution
in obedience and fear
of the authorities.

I believe in Jesus Christ
Who rises into our lives
in order that we may be freed
from prejudice and arrogance
from fear and hatred
and may carry forward his revolution
towards his kingdom.
I believe in the spirit
who came with Jesus into the world,
in the community of all nations
and in our responsibility
for what will become of our earth,
a valley of misery, starvation and violence
or the city of God.
I believe in just peace
which can be achieved
in the possibility of a meaningful life
for all people
in the future of this world of God.

Dorothee Sölle

4 *He gives me the strength to be daring, To build on him alone, for he shows himself as the ever greater One in my life.*

How did Mary find a sense of inner strength so that she was able to carry in her womb the developing life she believed came 'from God' and would one day present the world with a disturbing challenge? Her secret could help us to find true inner strength. She had long pondered the nature of the hidden mystery she had glimpsed in the gifts of the Magi: a new model of kingship (the leadership-in-service symbolised by gold given in a stable); the true worship of painful yet willing obedience (seen in the image of frankincense offered to a potential refugee); and the call to personal sacrifice – ultimate sacrifice if need be (the meaning of myrrh). This heady and potentially explosive combination somehow associated with the future adult life of the baby she was carrying meant that her role was decidedly 'daring'.

Such strength came from various components woven into a many-stranded cord. She was amazed by the way in which she had been singled out for this service and by her own daring answer, 'Yes.' She felt humble yet uplifted. God's choice of her in mercy and love was beyond her understanding but gave her special affirmation. Her swelling womb reminded her moment by moment of her calling to nurture a life that would uniquely focus service with obedience and sacrifice in a way that carried all the conviction of the power and presence of God. She realised that God's choice of her meant that while God loved everyone, his mercy especially regarded and resourced the overlooked and underprivileged of this world. He had shown this in the rescue of Hebrew slaves from hard labour in Egypt and in bringing them back from captivity in exile at a later date. In a similar way *our* sense of inner strength can come from a reborn sense of wonder, of personal involvement in God's loving intentions; the perception that we are 'seen' rather than overlooked and the assurance that God's mercies are not all in the past!

The freedom to be daring rather than letting life wear us down is expressed by T. S. Eliot in his poem, 'The Love Song of J. Alfred Prufrock'. Prufrock wonders how to challenge all the dull expectations by which life seems to conspire to put him down.

> And indeed there will be time
> To wonder, 'Do I dare?' and, 'Do I dare?'

> Time to turn back and descend the stair,
> With a bald spot in the middle of my hair –

As his spirit of ageing rebellion grows his urge to nonconformity brings him to the almost ridiculous:

> I grow old . . . I grow old . . .
> I shall wear the bottoms of my trousers rolled.

The lingering question for us is how we can harness the energy of youthful, middle-aged or later rebellion for worthwhile causes rather than lose it in futile gestures?

Potential embarrassment, public misunderstanding and condemnation *can* be out-faced in a non-defensive way if we have a sense of God-given worth. Discovering our lives to be rooted in God is an important personal breakthrough in a society where people tend to be affirmed by job title, money (or the show of money) and kudos. To possess a personal integrity that does not depend on public applause, hitting the headlines or 'hype' is a secure base worth having. The uncovering of this secure base on which to build the holy/whole life means letting go and more letting go! At first it is difficult to live without a daily fix of compliments, social buzz and pumping adrenalin. However, it is possible to pass a 'pain barrier' and discover a basis of life which is securely built on God. This does not mean that it is wrong to encourage people to praise one another more than they tend to do or that it is wrong to benefit from adrenalin in pressurised situations. But we learn not to *depend* on these daily shots in the arm. Instead we find support through the sustaining reality of what is known in Hebrew as 'hesed' – the overwhelming loving kindness and mercy of God by which alone we live.

Those who live in some houses built in the 1920s know that they can make lovely, spacious homes full of character, with features like bay windows, stained glass in hall windows and decorated plaster patterns on the ceilings. However, houses of this era are often built on surprisingly shallow foundations – poor footings that compare very unfavourably with modern specifications. Often this leads to the necessity for expensive 'underpinning' and all the mess and insurance-negotiation that go with such building operations. The costly and painful nature of finding our personal 'footing' should not be underestimated but the process is well worthwhile. It includes getting to know ourselves and our family heritage but mainly involves recognising God as the foundation of our being and seeing ourselves as contingent on him. Without this spiritual work of 'underpinning' all our comfortable 'show' will be just window dressing and we shall not be 'at home' to ourselves of God.

A pregnancy becomes more and more evident during its nine months. Similarly God's presence in our lives should become more detectable as faith helps us to 'embody' Christ. As we let go of previously prevailing self-interest and allow the quest for God's purposes to grow in our desires we develop a new way of thinking and a new set of priorities. Instinctive reactions like 'What shall I get out of this?' or 'How will this look on my CV?' are gradually replaced with questions like 'What does God want me to do in this situation?' or 'How will this course of action affect or benefit others?' Some people worry that this shift of focus and emphasis will make them into non-persons. That can only happen if the process goes wrong and spirals downwards into negative thinking so that everyone else matters and we don't seem to count! In this change of emphasis we find new fulfilment in and through our personal concern for others, and in prayerful choices about the way this is expressed.

We remain *real* people because we are caught up in larger concerns than our own selfish ends. Nonetheless we need enough personal space, fulfilment and solitude to enable us to reach out to others and achieve some balance of caring. We become spiritual commuters between solitude and the crowd, aloneness and involvement. The precise mix will be different for each of us according to temperament and spiritual make-up. The balance is struck as we write in the margin of our lives as J. S. Bach wrote on his music manuscripts: S. D. G. (Soli Deo Gloria – To God alone the glory); or J. J. (Jesu Juva – Help me, Jesus).

Discussion Starters

1. How can we distinguish between the revolution involved in preparing for the kingdom and pointless change for change's sake?

2. How can we be more 'rooted' in God for fulfilment instead of relying on pressure and praise to provide daily adrenalin?

3. How can we commute between the hilltop of inspiration and the valley of public demands?

John Walker

You asked for my hands
that you might use them for your purpose.
I gave them for a moment then withdrew them
for the work was hard.

You asked for my mouth
to speak out against injustice.
I gave you a whisper that I might not be accused.

You asked for my eyes
to see the pain of poverty.
I closed them for I did not want to see.

You asked for my life
that you might work through me.
I gave a small part that I might not get too involved.

Lord, forgive my calculated efforts to serve you,
only when it is convenient for me to do so,
only in those places where it is safe to do so,
and only with those who make it easy to do so.

Father, forgive me,
renew me
send me out
as a usable instrument
that I might take seriously
the meaning of your cross.

Joe Seremane

We thought we knew where to find you;
we hardly needed a star to guide the way,
just perseverance and common sense;
why do you hide yourself away from the powerful
and join the refugees and outcasts,
calling us to follow you there?
> *Wise God, give us wisdom.*

We thought we had laid you safe in the manger;
we wrapped you in the thickest sentiment we could find,
and stressed how long ago you came to us;
why do you break upon us in our daily life
with messages of peace and goodwill,
demanding that we do something about it?
> *Just and righteous God, give us justice and righteousness.*

So where else would we expect to find you
but in the ordinary place with the faithful people,
turning the world to your purpose through them.
Bring us to that manger, to that true rejoicing,
which will make wisdom, justice and righteousness alive in us.

Stephen Orchard

Sometimes the only right response is
Anger. Not dull resentment,
Poisoning all it touches, or
Bitterness that taints the memory,
But a clean cutting edge, that
Lances festering grievances,
Releasing energy to fight;
The fuel of passion that
Challenges evils,
Outwardly observed
Or known within.

Such anger is not sin.

Ann Lewin

Revolution is . . .

revolution is . . .
>   when the first ray of light
>   slashes night and day asunder

revolution is . . .
>   when a woman gives birth
>   with her thumb raised high
>   urging 'Amandla!'*

revolution is . . .
>   when a child marches from a womb
>   with a raised clenched fist
>   saying 'mama we are on our own!'

revolution is . . .
>   when consciousness tear the mask
>   hiding my sister's beautiful face
>   redeeming her blackness

revolution is . . .
>   when pick-axes and ploughs
>   pause to determine the worth
>   of sweat on labouring backs

revolution is . . .
>   when a forest rises to sharpen
>   its branches like pencils
>   then poetry will inscribe
>   the song of the river in ink

Essop Patel

*freedom, of South African origin.

30

5 *He has made known to me this: It is in my being servant That it becomes possible For God's kingdom to break through Here and now.*

It can be fascinating to hear people speak of their Christian experience. What becomes very clear is that God treats us as individuals because we are so different. He gets his message across to us in a way that we can understand.

Mary heard God's word to her with a certain amount of trepidation. What did it mean? Why had she been chosen for such a special task? God had a role for her which would revolutionise her life but she was not sure that she wanted to accept the implications. Her response is a model of obedience: 'Here am I, the servant of the Lord; let it be with me according to your word.' In this acceptance of her role she was in a great succession of God's servants who had responded to his call. Abraham received his marching orders: 'Go from your country . . . to the land that I will show you.' Sarah found it difficult to accept that she could have a son with Abraham but God's promise was realised: 'Sarah conceived and bore Abraham a son in his old age.' Eli realised that the Lord was calling Samuel and he told the young lad to reply: 'Speak, for your servant is listening.' Jeremiah was given his commission: 'See, today I appoint you over nations and over kingdoms, to pluck up and pull down, to destroy and to overthrow, to build and to plant.' All in their own way heard God's call and faced the demanding responsibilities which God had laid upon them.

The early disciples had the same experience. Simon and Andrew were working as fishermen when they heard the call of Jesus: 'Come, follow me.' As Paul reflected on God's choice, he concluded: 'God chose what is foolish in the world to shame the wise . . . what is weak in the world to shame the strong.' He was making the point that God often chooses the most unlikely people to do his work. The first followers of Jesus seemed to have so little to offer but they achieved so much in obedience to God's will. Mary understood the immediate demands of God's call despite an understandable reluctance on her part to see herself in the role which he had mapped out for her. Like so many of God's servants she was given a ministry to the powerful. Through her openness to God she became a channel of his grace and power.

The New Testament writers remind us that gifts are given to individuals for the benefit of the Church and the world. The obedience of the individual in using their God-given gifts makes its mark on the community. In *True Spirituality*, Francis Schaeffer writes:

> Christianity is an individual thing, but it is not *only* an individual thing. There is to be true community, offering true spiritual and material help to each other.

Writers have often described Jesus as revolutionary and, although we recognise the truth in this description, we know that he was not a revolutionary in the generally accepted sense of that word. He disappointed some of his followers because he refused to overthrow his nation's rulers by force. When one of his followers wanted to defend him on his arrest in the Garden of Gethsemane, Jesus told him to put his sword back into its place for that was not his way. Yet within a short space of time the followers of Jesus were recognised as revolutionaries who were turning the world upside down. Why? Part of the answer is that the coming of God's kingdom inevitably results in a political and social revolution as ordinary lives are tuned to do God's will. Paul preached: 'Christ nailed to the cross; and though this is an offence to Jews and folly to Gentiles, yet to those who are called, Jews and Greeks alike, he is the power of God and the wisdom of God.'

So often in times of human weakness and hesitation, God's presence is revealed and we catch glimpses of his kingdom, where ordinary lives become open to his will. The Bible stories offer examples of those who responded to God's call and who felt so unworthy and ill-equipped for the tasks they had been given. Moses asks: 'Who am I? . . . What shall I say?' Jeremiah protests: 'Truly I do not know how to speak, for I am only a boy.' Mary must have wondered how the voicing of her experience in the Magnificat would be received but she was prepared to trust the one who had called her to such a great purpose.

What is our understanding of God's kingdom? The teaching of Jesus suggests that there is a past, a present and a future dimension. In Mark's Gospel Jesus begins his ministry with the words: 'The time is fulfilled, and the kingdom of God has come near; repent and believe in the good news.' The kingdom is already present in the words and works of Jesus during his earthly ministry. However, this is not the end of the story, for many of Jesus' sayings look forward to a kingdom which is yet to come. At the Last Supper, Jesus shared the bread and wine with his disciples and said: 'I tell you, I will never again drink of this fruit of the vine until that day when I drink it with you in my Father's kingdom.' This tension between the present reality and the future fulfilment is clearly present in Jesus' teaching and has been interpreted in a variety of ways. In his letter to the Colossians, Paul speaks of the God who 'has rescued us from the power of darkness and transferred us into the kingdom of his beloved Son, in whom we have redemption, the forgiveness of sins'. This teaching about the past, the present reality and the future hope illustrates the radical transformation which lies at the heart of the Christian faith.

As Mary was the bearer of the Word of God, so the Church is called to bear that word for all. The deep humility of Mary is an example to the Church as it goes about its work. There can be no doubting God's promises. He has shown his faithfulness in the past. Mary knew that he would be true to his word and the Church must obediently accept its calling in Christ.

Discussion Starters:

1. How does God make himself known to us? Through creation? The Bible? Worship? Silence? Other people?

2. How does God's kingdom break through?

3. How 'revolting' are we called to be?

David Willie

Jesus
gift of God
to a worn-out world,
     let your presence
     open our eyes
     to see your salvation.

Jesus
gift of God
to a violent world,
     let your presence
     guide our feet
     into the way of peace.

Jesus
gift of God
to an unprepared world,
     let your presence
     rouse our sleeping spirits
     into welcome and worship.

Jesus
gift of God
to a rebellious world,
     let your presence
     confront our disobedience,
     redirecting our lives
     and transforming our society.

Jesus
Christmas gift
to us and the world,
     we offer you our lives
     that they in turn
     may be a gift to your world
     for its peace, its joy, its future
     displaying for all time
     your self-emptying pilgrimage to power and glory.

David Jenkins

Epilogue

The Nunc Dimittis (The Song of Simeon) provides an appropriate closing meditation for this book. Here an old man praises God that all his hopes are gloriously fulfilled in the Christ child.

Now, Lord, you let your servant go in peace:
your word has been fulfilled.

Simeon sees in Jesus the salvation which God offers to his people. This very public presentation in the Temple is for Simeon a sign of God's faithfulness. God has promised his people a deliverer and that promise is fulfilled in the coming of Jesus.

My own eyes have seen the salvation
which you have prepared in the sight of every people:

Simeon recognises that the salvation revealed in Jesus is not only for the people of Israel but is for all. The promise made to the nation of Israel as the chosen people of God is extended to all from every nation who are invited to live in the light of God's love as revealed by Jesus.

a light to reveal you to the nations
and the glory of your people Israel.

In a few moments of quietness let us thank God:

for all the ways in which he reveals himself to us;
for his faithfulness to the promises he has made;
for the salvation he has prepared for us in Jesus;
for his saving power revealed to all the world.

Glory to the Father, and to the Son,
and to the Holy Spirit:
as it was in the beginning,
is now, and shall be for ever. Amen.

Acknowledgements

Methodist Publishing House gratefully acknowledges permission to use copyright items. Every effort has been made to trace copyright owners, but where we have been unsuccessful we would welcome information which would enable us to make appropriate acknowledgement in any reprint.

Front cover based on 'Annunciation' by William Congdon.

Scripture quotations, unless otherwise stated, are from the New Revised Standard Version of the Bible, copyright © 1989 by the Division of Christian Education of the National Council of the Churches of Christ in the United States of America.

The version of the Magnificat used in this publication is translated by Sr Olga Wanke IBVM from German.

11 Ann Lewin, *Candles and Kingfishers*, Methodist Publishing House, 1997.

12 *The Methodist Worship Book*, p23, Trustees for Methodist Church Purposes, 1999.

12 Janet Morley, *Companions of God*, a Christian Aid Prayer Book, SPCK.

17 Kate Compston, *Encounters*, The Prayer Handbook for 1988, The United Reformed Church in the United Kingdom.

18 *Bread of Tomorrow*, SPCK and Christian Aid, 1992.

23 Janet Morley, *Bread of Tomorrow*, SPCK and Christian Aid, 1992.

23 Dorothy Sölle, 'Creed of Transformation', *Liturgy of Life*, National Christian Education Council.

26 T. S. Eliot, 'The Love Song of J. Alfred Prufock', *Collected Poems 1909-1962*, Faber and Faber Ltd.

28 Joe Seremane, *Bread of Tomorrow*, SPCK and Christian Aid, 1992.

29 Stephen Orchard, *All the Glorious Names*, The Prayer Handbook for 1989, The United Reformed Church in the United Kingdom.

29 Ann Lewin, *Candles and Kingfishers*, Methodist Publishing House, 1997.

32 Frances Schaeffer,*True Spirituality*, Send The Light 1979.

34 David Jenkins, *The Power and the Glory*, The Prayer Handbook for 1987, The United Reformed Church in the United Kingdom.

Let's Be Revolting brings together a series of new meditations on the Magnificat. The contributors believe that we cannot simply rest in the personal assurance of God's love and salvation, crucial though that is. We are called, as Mary was, to be among those who help to change the world, to prepare the way for God to bring in the Kingdom. We are indeed called 'to be revolting' in God's Name, on behalf of all those who feel themselves to be beyond God's love, or who are disadvantaged in any way.

ISBN 1-85852-128-9

9 781858 521282

PD465

Published by Methodist Publishing House
20 Ivatt Way
Peterborough PE3 7PG